Sparks
OF
Gratitude

This journal belongs to:

_____

_____

_____

igniumpress
www.authorsignite.com

Want a freebie?

Email us at
info@authorsignite.com.
Title the email *"Gratitude"* and
we'll send you something fun.

**Begin and end each day
with a grateful heart.**

It's a magnet for miracles.

Shop for more products like the
Sparks of Gratitude journal at
www.AuthorsIgnite.com/products.
Please keep our journals in mind for your
gift-giving needs. If you enjoyed this journal,
we would appreciate a positive review.
Thank you for your support
of our small business.

Debra Brown, Meredith Brown, and Jessica Nash

ISBN: 978-1-7341456-3-2

igniumpress

DESIGNED AND MADE IN THE USA

Welcome

There's power in appreciation and gratitude. This combination reduces stress, overcomes fear, makes you happier, and shows you solutions you never realized were possible.

If you commit to discovering the sparks of positivity in your daily life, you will be amazed at the difference in your attitude, drive, and success. Once you notice these sparks and appreciate them, you can be thankful for each one.

Melody Beatty says, "Gratitude makes sense of our past, brings peace for today, and creates a vision for tomorrow." Voltaire reminds us that "Appreciation is a wonderful thing. It makes what is excellent in others belong to us as well."

Use this gratitude journal to spark your appreciation of the positive things in your personal and professional life. Record 3 things you are grateful for daily, and refer back to them when you need to ignite your excitement, enthusiasm, and momentum. If you are struggling to think of one, flip back to the *Start Your Week... and End Your Week with Gratitude* prompts to jog your memory.

ENGAGE ● ELEVATE ● EMPOWER

Make the most of yourself
by fanning the tiny, inner

of possibilty into

of ACHIEVEMENT

GOLDA MEIR

SKETCHES, NOTES, IDEAS, LISTS,
THOUGHTS, DREAMS, HOPES,
PLANS, GOALS, POSSIBILITIES...

Start your week with  Gratitude

- ☐ Why you are grateful to be alive.
- ☐ Lessons learned.
- ☐ Positive things happening now.
- ☐ Your best skill.
- ☐ Favorite places to visit.
- ☐ Modern conveniences you appreciate.
- ☐ The colors and textures of nature.
- ☐ Your favorite meal.
- ☐ The feel of a hot shower on a cold day.
- ☐ Your talents.
- ☐ A cold drink on a hot day.
- ☐ The view out your window.
- ☐ A good book.
- ☐ A favorite sport.
- ☐ A friend you can count on no matter what.
- ☐ A fond memory.
- ☐ A letter you sent or received.
- ☐ Things money can't buy.
- ☐ Your favorite childhood memory.
- ☐ A favorite pet.
- ☐ Challenges that led to career growth.
- ☐ A funny story.
- ☐ Personal hurdles you conquered.
- ☐ A favorite hobby.
- ☐ Favorite birthday.
- ☐ A chat with friends.

- [ ] Struggles that led to strength.
- [ ] A favorite song.
- [ ] Someone you have forgiven.
- [ ] Luxuries you enjoy.
- [ ] Longtime friends.
- [ ] Best card you ever received or sent.
- [ ] A favorite movie.
- [ ] Your current goals.
- [ ] Your favorite coffee or tea.
- [ ] The sounds you hear.
- [ ] Things that relax you.
- [ ] Reasons to get up in the morning.
- [ ] Your best compliment.
- [ ] A recommendation by a peer.
- [ ] Your best vacation.
- [ ] A place on your bucket list.
- [ ] The best gift you received.
- [ ] Random kindness.
- [ ] Someone who made you smile.
- [ ] Art that moved you.
- [ ] Your best friend's qualities.
- [ ] Things you can control.
- [ ] A good workout.
- [ ] A walk on the beach.
- [ ] Your first snow.
- [ ] Simple pleasures.

End your week with *Gratitude*

I am grateful for: Date:

_____

_____

_____

I am grateful for: Date:

_____

_____

_____

I am grateful for: Date:

_____

_____

_____

I am grateful for: Date:

_____

_____

_____

Wear *gratitude* like a cloak, and it will feed every corner of your life.

RUMI

I am grateful for: Date:

_____
_____
_____

I am grateful for: Date:

_____
_____
_____

I am grateful for: Date:

_____
_____
_____

I am *thankful* for my greatest achievement this week.

I am grateful for: Date:

_____

_____

_____

I am grateful for: Date:

_____

_____

_____

I am grateful for: Date:

_____

_____

_____

I am grateful for: Date:

_____

_____

" The greatest gift that you
can give to others is the gift of
unconditional *love* and *acceptance*.

"

BRIAN TRACY

I am grateful for: Date:

_____

_____

_____

I am grateful for: Date:

_____

_____

_____

I am grateful for: Date:

_____

_____

_____

I am *thankful* for my greatest achievement this week.

I am grateful for: Date:

_____

_____

_____

I am grateful for: Date:

_____

_____

_____

I am grateful for: Date:

_____

_____

_____

I am grateful for: Date:

_____

_____

_____

> **"** We have only this moment, sparkling like a *star* in our hand, and melting like a *snowflake*. **"**

SIR FRANCIS BACON, SR

I am grateful for: Date:

_____

_____

_____

I am grateful for: Date:

_____

_____

_____

I am grateful for: Date:

_____

_____

_____

I am *thankful* for my greatest achievement this week.

Sparks OF Gratitude

I am grateful for: Date:

_____

_____

_____

I am grateful for: Date:

_____

_____

_____

I am grateful for: Date:

_____

_____

_____

I am grateful for: Date:

_____

_____

_____

The real gift of gratitude
is that the more *grateful*
you are, the more
present you become.

ROBERT HOLDEN

I am grateful for: Date:

_____

_____

_____

I am grateful for: Date:

_____

_____

_____

I am grateful for: Date:

_____

_____

_____

I am *thankful* for my greatest achievement this week.

I am grateful for: Date:

_____

_____

_____

I am grateful for: Date:

_____

_____

_____

I am grateful for: Date:

_____

_____

_____

I am grateful for: Date:

_____

_____

_____

> Be happy with what
> you've got while *working*
> for what you want.

HELEN KELLER

I am grateful for: Date:

_____

_____

_____

I am grateful for: Date:

_____

_____

_____

I am grateful for: Date:

_____

_____

_____

I am *thankful* for my greatest achievement this week.

I am grateful for: Date:

_____

_____

_____

I am grateful for: Date:

_____

_____

_____

I am grateful for: Date:

_____

_____

_____

I am grateful for: Date:

_____

_____

_____

Practicing *gratitude* is how we acknowledge that there's enough and we're enough. 99

BRENÉ BROWN

I am grateful for: Date:

_____

_____

_____

I am grateful for: Date:

_____

_____

_____

I am grateful for: Date:

_____

_____

_____

I am *thankful* for my greatest achievement this week.

I am grateful for: Date:

_____

_____

_____

I am grateful for: Date:

_____

_____

_____

I am grateful for: Date:

_____

_____

_____

I am grateful for: Date:

_____

_____

_____

One can never pay in *gratitude*; one can only pay 'in kind' somewhere else in life.

ANNE MORROW LINDBERGH

I am grateful for: Date:

_____

_____

_____

I am grateful for: Date:

_____

_____

_____

I am grateful for: Date:

_____

_____

_____

I am *thankful* for my greatest achievement this week.

I am grateful for: Date:

_____

_____

_____

I am grateful for: Date:

_____

_____

_____

I am grateful for: Date:

_____

_____

_____

I am grateful for: Date:

_____

_____

_____

" Create the habit of *gratitude* and watch your life *transform*.

"

ROBIN LEE

I am grateful for: Date:

_____

_____

_____

I am grateful for: Date:

_____

_____

_____

I am grateful for: Date:

_____

_____

_____

I am *thankful* for my greatest achievement this week.

I am grateful for: Date:

_____

_____

_____

I am grateful for: Date:

_____

_____

_____

I am grateful for: Date:

_____

_____

_____

I am grateful for: Date:

_____

_____

_____

> # This is a *wonderful* day.
> # I've never seen this one before.

MAYA ANGELOU

I am grateful for: Date:

_____

_____

_____

I am grateful for: Date:

_____

_____

_____

I am grateful for: Date:

_____

_____

_____

I am *thankful* for my greatest achievement this week.

I am grateful for: Date:

_____

_____

_____

I am grateful for: Date:

_____

_____

_____

I am grateful for: Date:

_____

_____

_____

I am grateful for: Date:

_____

_____

_____

" **Gratitude** is the rich soil you plant your **future** in. "

LISA NICHOLS

I am grateful for: Date:

_____

_____

_____

I am grateful for: Date:

_____

_____

_____

I am grateful for: Date:

_____

_____

_____

I am *thankful* for my greatest achievement this week.

From a little

spark

may burst a

flame

DANTE ALIGHIERI

SKETCHES, NOTES, IDEAS, LISTS,
THOUGHTS, DREAMS, HOPES,
PLANS, GOALS, POSSIBILITIES...

I am grateful for: Date:

_____

_____

_____

I am grateful for: Date:

_____

_____

_____

I am grateful for: Date:

_____

_____

_____

I am grateful for: Date:

_____

_____

_____

Think with deep gratitude of those who lighted the *flame* within us.

ALBERT SCHWEITZER

I am grateful for: Date:

_____

_____

_____

I am grateful for: Date:

_____

_____

_____

I am grateful for: Date:

_____

_____

_____

I am *thankful* for my greatest achievement this week.

Sparks OF Gratitude

I am grateful for: Date:

_____

_____

_____

I am grateful for: Date:

_____

_____

_____

I am grateful for: Date:

_____

_____

_____

I am grateful for: Date:

_____

_____

_____

Happiness is when what you *think*,
what you *say*, and what you *do* are
in harmony.

MAHATMA GANDHI

I am grateful for: Date:

_____

_____

_____

I am grateful for: Date:

_____

_____

_____

I am grateful for: Date:

_____

_____

_____

I am *thankful* for my greatest achievement this week.

I am grateful for: Date:

_____

_____

_____

I am grateful for: Date:

_____

_____

_____

I am grateful for: Date:

_____

_____

_____

I am grateful for: Date:

_____

_____

_____

" Feeling *gratitude* and not *expressing* it is like wrapping a present and not giving it. **"**

WILLIAM ARTHUR WARD

I am grateful for: Date:

_____

_____

_____

I am grateful for: Date:

_____

_____

_____

I am grateful for: Date:

_____

_____

_____

I am *thankful* for my greatest achievement this week.

I am grateful for: Date:

_____

_____

_____

I am grateful for: Date:

_____

_____

_____

I am grateful for: Date:

_____

_____

_____

I am grateful for: Date:

_____

_____

_____

> " It is through gratitude for the ***present*** moment that the ***spiritual*** dimension of life opens up. "

ECKHART TOLLE

I am grateful for: Date:

_____

_____

_____

I am grateful for: Date:

_____

_____

_____

I am grateful for: Date:

_____

_____

_____

I am *thankful* for my greatest achievement this week.

Sparks OF Gratitude

I am grateful for: Date:

_____

_____

_____

I am grateful for: Date:

_____

_____

_____

I am grateful for: Date:

_____

_____

_____

I am grateful for: Date:

_____

_____

_____

" Among the things you can give and still keep are your *word*, a *smile*, and a *grateful heart*. **"**

ZIG ZIGLAR

I am grateful for: Date:

_____

_____

_____

I am grateful for: Date:

_____

_____

_____

I am grateful for: Date:

_____

_____

_____

I am *thankful* for my greatest achievement this week.

I am grateful for: Date:

_____

_____

_____

I am grateful for: Date:

_____

_____

_____

I am grateful for: Date:

_____

_____

_____

I am grateful for: Date:

_____

_____

_____

" Happiness doesn't depend on any external conditions, it is governed by our *mental attitude*. "

DALE CARNEGIE

I am grateful for: Date:

_____

_____

_____

I am grateful for: Date:

_____

_____

_____

I am grateful for: Date:

_____

_____

_____

I am *thankful* for my greatest achievement this week.

I am grateful for: Date:

_____

_____

_____

I am grateful for: Date:

_____

_____

_____

I am grateful for: Date:

_____

_____

_____

I am grateful for: Date:

_____

_____

_____

> Sometimes the *best things* are right in front of you; it just takes some time to *see* them. **99**

GLADYS KNIGHT

I am grateful for: Date:

_____

_____

_____

I am grateful for: Date:

_____

_____

_____

I am grateful for: Date:

_____

_____

_____

I am *thankful* for my greatest achievement this week.

Sparks OF Gratitude

I am grateful for: Date:

_____

_____

_____

I am grateful for: Date:

_____

_____

_____

I am grateful for: Date:

_____

_____

_____

I am grateful for: Date:

_____

_____

_____

" **Happiness** is not something
you postpone for the future;
it is something you **design**
for the present. *"*

JIM ROHN

I am grateful for: Date:

_____

_____

_____

I am grateful for: Date:

_____

_____

_____

I am grateful for: Date:

_____

_____

_____

I am *thankful* for my greatest achievement this week.

I am grateful for: Date:

_____

_____

_____

I am grateful for: Date:

_____

_____

_____

I am grateful for: Date:

_____

_____

_____

I am grateful for: Date:

_____

_____

_____

> Gratitude changes the pangs of memory into a *tranquil joy*.

DIETRICH BONHOFFER

I am grateful for: Date:

_____

_____

_____

I am grateful for: Date:

_____

_____

_____

I am grateful for: Date:

_____

_____

_____

I am *thankful* for my greatest achievement this week.

I am grateful for: Date:

_____

_____

_____

I am grateful for: Date:

_____

_____

_____

I am grateful for: Date:

_____

_____

_____

I am grateful for: Date:

_____

_____

_____

> **"** When people are generally *happy* with the success of others, the pie gets *larger*. **"**

STEPHEN COVEY

I am grateful for: Date:

_____

_____

_____

I am grateful for: Date:

_____

_____

_____

I am grateful for: Date:

_____

_____

_____

I am *thankful* for my greatest achievement this week.

IMAGINATION
is the
spark
that IGNITES the
fire of CREATIVITY

RICHARD L PETERSON

SKETCHES, NOTES, IDEAS, LISTS,
THOUGHTS, DREAMS, HOPES,
PLANS, GOALS, POSSIBILITIES...

I am grateful for: Date:

_____

_____

_____

I am grateful for: Date:

_____

_____

_____

I am grateful for: Date:

_____

_____

_____

I am grateful for: Date:

_____

_____

_____

" The art of being happy lies in the power of *extracting happiness* from common things. "

HENRY WARD BEECHER

I am grateful for: Date:

_____

_____

_____

I am grateful for: Date:

_____

_____

_____

I am grateful for: Date:

_____

_____

_____

I am *thankful* for my greatest achievement this week.

I am grateful for: Date:

_____

_____

_____

I am grateful for: Date:

_____

_____

_____

I am grateful for: Date:

_____

_____

_____

I am grateful for: Date:

_____

_____

_____

> ❝ The more you *praise* and *celebrate* your life, the more *you* there is in life to celebrate. ❞

DAVID STEINDL-RAST

I am grateful for: Date:

_____
_____
_____

I am grateful for: Date:

_____
_____
_____

I am grateful for: Date:

_____
_____
_____

I am *thankful* for my greatest achievement this week.

I am grateful for: Date:

_____

_____

_____

I am grateful for: Date:

_____

_____

_____

I am grateful for: Date:

_____

_____

_____

I am grateful for: Date:

_____

_____

_____

> Shine *brightly*. See *beauty*. Speak *kindly*. Love *truly*. Give *freely*. Create *joyfully*. Live *thankfully*.

MARY DAVIS

I am grateful for: Date:

_____

_____

_____

I am grateful for: Date:

_____

_____

_____

I am grateful for: Date:

_____

_____

_____

I am *thankful* for my greatest achievement this week.

I am grateful for: Date:

_____

_____

_____

I am grateful for: Date:

_____

_____

_____

I am grateful for: Date:

_____

_____

_____

I am grateful for: Date:

_____

_____

_____

Life is a *dance*. Mindfulness is witnessing that dance.

AMIT RAY

I am grateful for: Date:

_____

_____

_____

I am grateful for: Date:

_____

_____

_____

I am grateful for: Date:

_____

_____

_____

I am *thankful* for my greatest achievement this week.

I am grateful for: Date:

_____

_____

_____

I am grateful for: Date:

_____

_____

_____

I am grateful for: Date:

_____

_____

_____

I am grateful for: Date:

_____

_____

_____

"
Enjoy the *little things*, for one
day you may look back and realize
they were the *big things*.
"

ROBERT BRAULT

I am grateful for: Date:

_____

_____

_____

I am grateful for: Date:

_____

_____

_____

I am grateful for: Date:

_____

_____

_____

I am *thankful* for my greatest achievement this week.

I am grateful for: Date:

_____

_____

_____

I am grateful for: Date:

_____

_____

_____

I am grateful for: Date:

_____

_____

_____

I am grateful for: Date:

_____

_____

_____

If you want to find *happiness;* find *gratitude.*

STEVE MARIBOLI

I am grateful for: Date:

_____

_____

_____

I am grateful for: Date:

_____

_____

_____

I am grateful for: Date:

_____

_____

_____

I am *thankful* for my greatest achievement this week.

I am grateful for: Date:

_____

_____

_____

I am grateful for: Date:

_____

_____

_____

I am grateful for: Date:

_____

_____

_____

I am grateful for: Date:

_____

_____

_____

No duty is more *urgent* than that of returning *thanks*.

JAMES ALLEN

I am grateful for: Date:

_____

_____

_____

I am grateful for: Date:

_____

_____

_____

I am grateful for: Date:

_____

_____

_____

I am *thankful* for my greatest achievement this week.

I am grateful for: Date:

_____

_____

_____

I am grateful for: Date:

_____

_____

_____

I am grateful for: Date:

_____

_____

_____

I am grateful for: Date:

_____

_____

_____

> # Don't count the days.
> # Make the *days count*.

MOHAMMED ALI

I am grateful for: Date:

_____

_____

_____

I am grateful for: Date:

_____

_____

_____

I am grateful for: Date:

_____

_____

_____

I am *thankful* for my greatest achievement this week.

I am grateful for: Date:

_____

_____

_____

I am grateful for: Date:

_____

_____

_____

I am grateful for: Date:

_____

_____

_____

I am grateful for: Date:

_____

_____

_____

We must *always* be on the *lookout* for the presence of *wonder*.

E.B. WHITE

I am grateful for: Date:

_____

_____

_____

I am grateful for: Date:

_____

_____

_____

I am grateful for: Date:

_____

_____

_____

I am *thankful* for my greatest achievement this week.

I am grateful for: Date:

_____
_____
_____

I am grateful for: Date:

_____
_____
_____

I am grateful for: Date:

_____
_____
_____

I am grateful for: Date:

_____
_____
_____

There is a *fuel* in us which needs to be *ignited* with *sparks*.

JOHANN GOTTFRIED HERDER

I am grateful for: Date:

_____

_____

_____

I am grateful for: Date:

_____

_____

_____

I am grateful for: Date:

_____

_____

_____

I am *thankful* for my greatest achievement this week.

I am grateful for: Date:

_____

_____

_____

I am grateful for: Date:

_____

_____

_____

I am grateful for: Date:

_____

_____

_____

I am grateful for: Date:

_____

_____

_____

There are far, far *better things* ahead than any we *leave behind*.

C.S. LEWIS

I am grateful for: Date:

_____

_____

_____

I am grateful for: Date:

_____

_____

_____

I am grateful for: Date:

_____

_____

_____

I am *thankful* for my greatest achievement this week.

A *spark*

is a little thing,

yet it may

kindle

the WORLD.

MARTIN FARQUHAR TUPPER

SKETCHES, NOTES, IDEAS, LISTS,
THOUGHTS, DREAMS, HOPES,
PLANS, GOALS, POSSIBILITIES...

I am grateful for: Date:

_____

_____

_____

I am grateful for: Date:

_____

_____

_____

I am grateful for: Date:

_____

_____

_____

I am grateful for: Date:

_____

_____

_____

Be *patient* and ***tough***. Someday
this pain will be useful to you.

OVID

I am grateful for: Date:

_____

_____

_____

I am grateful for: Date:

_____

_____

_____

I am grateful for: Date:

_____

_____

_____

I am *thankful* for my greatest achievement this week.

I am grateful for: Date:

_____

_____

_____

I am grateful for: Date:

_____

_____

_____

I am grateful for: Date:

_____

_____

_____

I am grateful for: Date:

_____

_____

_____

We are such stuff as *dreams* are made of.

WILLIAM SHAKESPEARE

I am grateful for: Date:

_____

_____

_____

I am grateful for: Date:

_____

_____

_____

I am grateful for: Date:

_____

_____

_____

I am *thankful* for my greatest achievement this week.

I am grateful for: Date:

_____

_____

_____

I am grateful for: Date:

_____

_____

_____

I am grateful for: Date:

_____

_____

_____

I am grateful for: Date:

_____

_____

_____

"

Start where you are.
Use what you have.
Do what you can.

,,

ARTHUR ASHE

I am grateful for: Date:

_____

_____

_____

I am grateful for: Date:

_____

_____

_____

I am grateful for: Date:

_____

_____

_____

I am *thankful* for my greatest achievement this week.

I am grateful for: Date:

_____

_____

_____

I am grateful for: Date:

_____

_____

_____

I am grateful for: Date:

_____

_____

_____

I am grateful for: Date:

_____

_____

_____

An awake *heart* is like a *sky* that pours *light*.

HAFEZ

I am grateful for: Date:

_____

_____

_____

I am grateful for: Date:

_____

_____

_____

I am grateful for: Date:

_____

_____

_____

I am *thankful* for my greatest achievement this week.

Sparks OF Gratitude

I am grateful for: Date:

_____

_____

_____

I am grateful for: Date:

_____

_____

_____

I am grateful for: Date:

_____

_____

_____

I am grateful for: Date:

_____

_____

_____

The sun shines not
on us, but *in* us.

JOHN MUIR

I am grateful for: Date:

_____

_____

_____

I am grateful for: Date:

_____

_____

_____

I am grateful for: Date:

_____

_____

_____

I am *thankful* for my greatest achievement this week.

I am grateful for: Date:

_____
_____
_____

I am grateful for: Date:

_____
_____
_____

I am grateful for: Date:

_____
_____
_____

I am grateful for: Date:

_____
_____
_____

"

Dismiss whatever insults
your own *soul*.

"

WALT WHITMAN

I am grateful for: Date:

_____

_____

_____

I am grateful for: Date:

_____

_____

_____

I am grateful for: Date:

_____

_____

_____

I am *thankful* for my greatest achievement this week.

I am grateful for: Date:

_____

_____

_____

I am grateful for: Date:

_____

_____

_____

I am grateful for: Date:

_____

_____

_____

I am grateful for: Date:

_____

_____

_____

> ## No need to *hurry*, no need to *sparkle*, no need to be anyone but *one's self*.

I am grateful for: Date:

_____

_____

_____

I am grateful for: Date:

_____

_____

_____

I am grateful for: Date:

_____

_____

_____

I am *thankful* for my greatest achievement this week.

I am grateful for: Date:

_____

_____

_____

I am grateful for: Date:

_____

_____

_____

I am grateful for: Date:

_____

_____

_____

I am grateful for: Date:

_____

_____

_____

Those who have the ability
to be *grateful* are the
ones who have the ability
to achieve *greatness.* **99**

STEVE MARIBOLI

I am grateful for: Date:

_____

_____

_____

I am grateful for: Date:

_____

_____

_____

I am grateful for: Date:

_____

_____

_____

I am *thankful* for my greatest achievement this week.

I am grateful for: Date:

_____

_____

_____

I am grateful for: Date:

_____

_____

_____

I am grateful for: Date:

_____

_____

_____

I am grateful for: Date:

_____

_____

_____

" When it comes to life,
the *critical thing* is whether
you take things for *granted*
or take them with *gratitude*. **"**

G. K. CHESTERTON

I am grateful for: Date:

_____

_____

_____

I am grateful for: Date:

_____

_____

_____

I am grateful for: Date:

_____

_____

_____

I am *thankful* for my greatest achievement this week.

I am grateful for: Date:

_____

_____

_____

I am grateful for: Date:

_____

_____

_____

I am grateful for: Date:

_____

_____

_____

I am grateful for: Date:

_____

_____

_____

Things turn out best for people who *make the best* of the way things turn out.

JOHN WOODEN

I am grateful for: Date:

_____

_____

_____

I am grateful for: Date:

_____

_____

_____

I am grateful for: Date:

_____

_____

_____

I am *thankful* for my greatest achievement this week.

When *sparks fly,*
some truly
great ideas come to
light.

DAVID HEINEMEIER HANSSON

SKETCHES, NOTES, IDEAS, LISTS,
THOUGHTS, DREAMS, HOPES,
PLANS, GOALS, POSSIBILITIES...

I am grateful for: Date:

_____

_____

_____

I am grateful for: Date:

_____

_____

_____

I am grateful for: Date:

_____

_____

_____

I am grateful for: Date:

_____

_____

_____

"

When you are *grateful*, fear *disappears* and abundance *appears*.

"

TONY ROBBINS

I am grateful for: Date:

_____

_____

_____

I am grateful for: Date:

_____

_____

_____

I am grateful for: Date:

_____

_____

_____

I am *thankful* for my greatest achievement this week.

Sparks OF Gratitude

I am grateful for: Date:

_____

_____

_____

I am grateful for: Date:

_____

_____

_____

I am grateful for: Date:

_____

_____

_____

I am grateful for: Date:

_____

_____

_____

I am grateful for: Date:

_____

_____

_____

I am grateful for: Date:

_____

_____

_____

I am grateful for: Date:

_____

_____

_____

I am *thankful* for my greatest achievement this week.

I am grateful for: Date:

_____

_____

_____

I am grateful for: Date:

_____

_____

_____

I am grateful for: Date:

_____

_____

_____

I am grateful for: Date:

_____

_____

_____

> **"** You are what you think.
> So *think* big, *believe* big, *act* big, *work*
> big, *give* big, *forgive* big,
> *laugh* big, *love* big, and *live* big. **"**

ANDREW CARNEGIE

I am grateful for: Date:

_____

_____

_____

I am grateful for: Date:

_____

_____

_____

I am grateful for: Date:

_____

_____

_____

I am *thankful* for my greatest achievement this week.

I am grateful for: Date:

_____

_____

_____

I am grateful for: Date:

_____

_____

_____

I am grateful for: Date:

_____

_____

_____

I am grateful for: Date:

_____

_____

_____

Life can be seen through your *eyes* but it is not fully appreciated until it is seen through your *heart.* 99

MARY XAVIER MEHEGAN

I am grateful for: Date:

_____

_____

_____

I am grateful for: Date:

_____

_____

_____

I am grateful for: Date:

_____

_____

_____

I am *thankful* for my greatest achievement this week.

I am grateful for: Date:

_____

_____

_____

I am grateful for: Date:

_____

_____

_____

I am grateful for: Date:

_____

_____

_____

I am grateful for: Date:

_____

_____

_____

" Appreciation is a *wonderful* thing: it makes what is excellent in otherS *belong to us* as well. **"**

VOLTAIRE

I am grateful for: Date:

_____

_____

_____

I am grateful for: Date:

_____

_____

_____

I am grateful for: Date:

_____

_____

_____

I am *thankful* for my greatest achievement this week.

I am grateful for: Date:

_____

_____

_____

I am grateful for: Date:

_____

_____

_____

I am grateful for: Date:

_____

_____

_____

I am grateful for: Date:

_____

_____

_____

"

When we give *cheerfully*
and accept *gratefully*,
everyone is blessed.

"

MAYA ANGELOU

I am grateful for: Date:

_____

_____

_____

I am grateful for: Date:

_____

_____

_____

I am grateful for: Date:

_____

_____

_____

I am *thankful* for my greatest achievement this week.

Sparks of Gratitude

I am grateful for: Date:

_____

_____

_____

I am grateful for: Date:

_____

_____

_____

I am grateful for: Date:

_____

_____

_____

I am grateful for: Date:

_____

_____

_____

Relationships are based on four principles: *respect, understanding, acceptance,* and *appreciation.*

MAHATMA GANDHI

I am grateful for: Date:

_____

_____

_____

I am grateful for: Date:

_____

_____

_____

I am grateful for: Date:

_____

_____

_____

I am *thankful* for my greatest achievement this week.

I am grateful for: **Date:**

_____

_____

_____

I am grateful for: **Date:**

_____

_____

_____

I am grateful for: **Date:**

_____

_____

_____

I am grateful for: **Date:**

_____

_____

_____

"
There are two ways of *spreading light*: to be the *candle* or the *mirror* that reflects it.
"

EDITH WHARTON

I am grateful for: Date:

_____

_____

_____

I am grateful for: Date:

_____

_____

_____

I am grateful for: Date:

_____

_____

_____

I am *thankful* for my greatest achievement this week.

I am grateful for: Date:

_____

_____

_____

I am grateful for: Date:

_____

_____

_____

I am grateful for: Date:

_____

_____

_____

I am grateful for: Date:

_____

_____

_____

The **smallest** thanks is
always worth *more* than
the *effort* it takes to give it.

99

UNKNOWN

I am grateful for: Date:

_____

_____

_____

I am grateful for: Date:

_____

_____

_____

I am grateful for: Date:

_____

_____

_____

I am *thankful* for my greatest achievement this week.

I am grateful for: Date:

_____

_____

_____

I am grateful for: Date:

_____

_____

_____

I am grateful for: Date:

_____

_____

_____

I am grateful for: Date:

_____

_____

_____

> **Kindness** is more important than wisdom, and the recognition of this is the **beginning** of wisdom.

THEODORE ISAAC RUBIN

I am grateful for: Date:

_____

_____

_____

I am grateful for: Date:

_____

_____

_____

I am grateful for: Date:

_____

_____

_____

I am *thankful* for my greatest achievement this week.

I am grateful for: Date:

_____

_____

_____

I am grateful for: Date:

_____

_____

_____

I am grateful for: Date:

_____

_____

_____

I am grateful for: Date:

_____

_____

_____

When *nothing* is sure, everything is *possible*.

MARGARET DRABBLE

I am grateful for: Date:

_____

_____

_____

I am grateful for: Date:

_____

_____

_____

I am grateful for: Date:

_____

_____

_____

I am *thankful* for my greatest achievement this week.

A
*grateful
heart*

is a MAGNET for

miracles.

UNKNOWN

SKETCHES, NOTES, IDEAS, LISTS,
THOUGHTS, DREAMS, HOPES,
PLANS, GOALS, POSSIBILITIES...

Made in the USA
Columbia, SC
22 December 2020